VOICES OF WAR

The Afghanistan and Iraq Wars
War Against Extremism

Enzo George

Cavendish Square

New York

Published in 2015 by Cavendish Square Publishing, LLC
243 5th Avenue, Suite 136, New York, NY 10016

© 2015 Brown Bear Books Ltd

First Edition

Website: cavendishsq.com

CPSIA Compliance Information: Batch #WS14CSQ

All websites were available and accurate when this book was sent to press.

Library of Congress Cataloging-in-Publication Data
George, Enzo.
The Afghanistan and Iraq Wars: wars against extremism / by Enzo George.
p. cm. — (Voices of war)
Includes index.
ISBN 978-1-62712-879-7 (hardcover) ISBN 978-1-62712-881-0 (ebook)
1. Afghan War, 2001- — Juvenile literature. 2. Iraq War, 2003-2011 — Juvenile literature. 3. War on Terrorism, 2001-2009 — Juvenile literature. I. Title.
HV6431.G46 2015
956.7044—d23

For Brown Bear Books Ltd:
Editorial Director: Lindsey Lowe
Managing Editor: Tim Cooke
Children's Publisher: Anne O'Daly
Design Manager: Keith Davis
Designer: Lynne Lennon
Picture Manager: Sophie Mortimer
Production Director: Alastair Gourlay

Picture Credits:
Front Cover: U.S. Department of Defense

All images **U.S. Department of Defense** except:
Alamy: Enigma 30, Hisham Ibrahim/PhotoV 31; **Corbis:** Ron Haviv/VII 8, Mian Kursheed/X01147/Reuters 13; **Getty Images:** Karim Sahib/AFP 23; **Menendj:** 33; **Robert Hunt Library:** 12; **Shutterstock:** Anthony Correia 7, Ken Tannenbaum 6; **U.S. Federal Government:** 44.

Artistic Effects: Shutterstock

Brown Bear Books has made every attempt to contact the copyright holder. If you have any information please contact licensing@windmillbooks.co.uk

We believe the extracts included in this book to be material in the public domain. Anyone having any further information should contact licensing@windmillbooks.co.uk.

Manufactured in the United States of America

CONTENTS

Introduction

On September 11, 2001, terrorists hijacked four airliners and flew them into targets in the United States. The attacks were quickly linked to al-Qaeda, an extremist Islamic group that was based in Afghanistan. It was protected there by the Taliban government, which enforced a strict form of Islamic rule.

U.S. President George W. Bush declared a "war on terror." The United States assembled an international coalition to invade Afghanistan, where they soon drove out the Taliban. Most al-Qaeda in the country fled into neighboring Pakistan. Well over a decade after the invasion, however, the Taliban remained active, mainly in the remote Helmand province.

U.S. tanks in the streets of an Iraqi town. U.S. firepower was far greater than that of its enemies.

A U.S. soldier keeps guard during a patrol in Tarmiyah, Iraq, in May 2007.

A U.S. Marine sergeant from Female Engagement Team 3 leaves for a patrol in Afghanistan, February 2012.

In 2003 the war on terror shifted to Iraq. The Iraqi dictator, Saddam Hussein, was believed to possess chemical weapons that would allow him to strike at his neighbors. Some politicians also claimed that Saddam was linked to al-Qaeda, although most experts disagreed. Despite huge public protest around the world, the United States and its allies invaded Iraq and toppled Saddam.

Iraq descended into violence as Sunni and Shiite Muslims attacked each other—and Coalition forces. In 2007 the Americans launched a troop "surge" to end the violence. But Iraq had still not returned to peace by the time the last U.S. forces left the country in 2011.

Terror Attacks

On September 11, 2001, terrorists crashed four hijacked airliners into targets in the United States: two struck the World Trade Center in New York City; one hit the Pentagon in Washington, D.C.; and the other crashed into a field in Pennsylvania. In all, 2,977 victims were killed.

The attacks were carried out by Islamic extremists from the al-Qaeda organization. They took the United States by surprise. After the first plane hit the World Trade Center, emergency crews from all over New York rushed to the scene.

Smoke billows from one of the Twin Towers of the World Trade Center after the first plane struck.

Dust surrounds a fire truck after the towers collapsed. More than 340 firefighters died in the 9/11 attacks.

" We could visually see the upper floors of the World Trade Center emanating heavy smoke and fire… There was a lot of debris falling down. There was very heavy fire on the upper floors of the building…

We observed people jumping from the building, we observed debris falling from both buildings… This is after, naturally, the second plane had hit 2 World Trade Center, which happened while we were there…

At that point in time we heard a rumble, we heard a noise, and then the building came down. All we saw was dust and everything just started to get very chaotic. At that point in time all of us at the command post, firefighters, chiefs, myself, we turned around, we started to run south, down West Street toward Albany. "

New York Assistant Fire Commissioner Stephen Gregory was in his office when he heard police radio broadcasts about the attack on the World Trade Center. He gave this testimony to a hearing about the disaster on October 3, 2001.

TERROR ATTACK FACTS

- The terrorists had learned to fly at U.S. flying schools.
- The attacks were planned to cause maximum devastation and loss of life.
- The fourth plane failed to reach its target when passengers overpowered the terrorists and the aircraft crashed.
- Citizens of 80 countries died in the terrorist attacks.
- The blame was soon placed on the al-Qaeda organization led by the Saudi Osama bin-Laden.
- Al-Qaeda had attacked U.S. targets previously, including the World Trade Center in 1993.

Going to War

U.S. Secretary of State Colin Powell addresses the United Nations. Powell had served as a general in the Persian Gulf War (1990-1991).

Days after the 9/11 attacks, President George W. Bush announced that the United States would punish the organization behind them. The al-Qaeda group was based in Afghanistan, where it was protected by the extremist Taliban government. Backed by the United Nations (UN), the U.S. government assembled an international coalition. In January 2002 Bush announced the start of a global War on Terror.

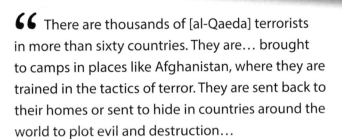

GOING TO WAR FACTS

- The North Alliance Treaty Organization (NATO) announced that the 9/11 attacks were an attack on all its members.
- President George W. Bush used the phrase "war on terror" for the first time in his address to Congress.
- U.S. and British jets began to bomb Afghanistan in October 2001, supported by a broad coalition of nations.
- The Taliban fled Afghanistan at the end of November 2001, but Osama bin Laden remained at large.
- President Bush officially began the "war on terror" in January 2002.

❝ There are thousands of [al-Qaeda] terrorists in more than sixty countries. They are… brought to camps in places like Afghanistan, where they are trained in the tactics of terror. They are sent back to their homes or sent to hide in countries around the world to plot evil and destruction…

Our war on terror begins with al-Qaeda, but it does not end there. It will not end until every terrorist group of global reach has been found, stopped and defeated… From this day forward, any nation that continues to harbor or support terrorism will be regarded by the United States as a hostile regime… Our nation has been put on notice: We are not immune from attack. We will take defensive measures against terrorism to protect Americans… Freedom and fear are at war. **❞**

President George W. Bush addresses Congress and the nation about the U.S. response to the terrorist attacks, September 20, 2001.

Canada and Other Allies

After the 9/11 attacks, many nations were ready to help defeat Osama bin Laden and the Taliban regime of Afghanistan. Under NATO supervision, the United States was joined by Britain, France, Canada, Australia, Denmark, and Germany. Inside Afghanistan, they were supported by the main opposition groups, a loose coalition of tribal warlords known as the Northern Alliance who wanted to overthrow the Taliban.

Afghan National Army officers meet French soldiers in Kapisa Province in February 2008.

❝ Freight and personnel were hustled off the plane to the Kandahar passenger terminal. The windows at the time had no glass. There were no lights except a hazy glow from floodlights that surrounded the prisoner compound…

We were shown where to set up our four-man tents, our quarters for the next six months or so. We slept on a cot and air mattress only when the sun went down; the air was too hot inside them otherwise. The compound we were to use was not cleared of mines; the engineers then had to cover it with crushed rock. When we did move into the compound we had to put sheets of wood down under our tents so they would not get torn up by the sharp rocks. Meals were Canadian IMPs (Individual Meal Packs) or American MREs (Meals Ready to Eat) as there were no mess halls. **❞**

Warrant Officer Randie Potts, of the 1st Service Battalion, Canadian Army, recalls arriving at Kandahar airport for duty in Afghanistan.

ALLIES FACTS

- Leading members of the NATO International Security Assistance Force included France, Great Britain, and Canada.
- NATO's mission statement was to rebuild Afghanistan once the Taliban government had been removed.
- The Canadian troops were based at Camp Julien.
- By February 2002, eighteen nations had sent troops or assistance to the UN force.
- By August 2003, 5,000 troops from more than thirty nations were present.
- By August 2013, there were 87,000 troops from 49 countries in Afghanistan.

French and U.S. soldiers cooperate during a training exercise for recruits to the Afghanistan Army.

The Enemy

The Taliban came to power in Afghanistan in 1998. They gave shelter to Osama bin Laden after al-Qaeda was expelled from Africa. After the 9/11 attacks President George W. Bush gave the Taliban an ultimatum to hand over Osama bin Laden. When they refused, Operation Enduring Freedom was launched on October 7, 2001. Al-Qaeda's leaders fled across the border to Pakistan.

Osama bin Laden came from a wealthy Saudi family. He formed al-Qaeda around 1989.

Armed members of the Taliban ride in the back of a pick-up truck. One carries a rocket-propeled grenade.

"" The enemy was brave and organized. In 2002, when I was over there, we had sporadic [occasional] encounters that were rarely reported or too minor to mention. They were disjointed. The attacks might be a rocket here or a gunshot there, but there were only three or four guys involved perhaps.

In 2006, from our vantage point, they were acting like a conventional army. They were moving to flanking positions in groups of thirty or forty. They probed to find out what assets we had, and then they'd move in. They were smart. And it was all by cell phones or by timings. They were moving in big groups, coordinated, and doing their attacks using contemporary Western doctrine on how to fight an army and crush them eventually. They knew where to shoot and they were good. They were a formidable army by then… These guys were fighting for something and they were determined to win. ""

Captain Derek David Prohar, a Canadian liaison officer with the U.S. Special Forces in Afghanistan, was awarded the Medal of Military Valour for his actions during the Battle of Sperwan Ghar.

THE ENEMY FACTS

- The Taliban believe in a strict version of Sharia, or Islamic law.
- Under Taliban rule, women had to wear a burka that covered their body and face. Girls over ten could not go to school. TV, music, and movies were banned.
- By 1998, the Taliban controlled almost 90 percent of Afghanistan.
- Al-Qaeda is a mainly Arab movement opposed to regimes in the Middle East.
- Al-Qaeda members in Afghanistan escaped across the border into Pakistan in December 2001.

Life in Afghanistan

This view shows part of the Forward Operating Base at Kandahar Airport. The small tents on the left are "bivouacs" for soldiers to sleep in.

The Allied mission in Afghanistan faced great difficulties. The huge country was full of mountains and deserts. Allied soldiers fought with pro-Western Afghans to remove al-Qaeda and the Taliban, but the enemy hid in remote caves and mountains. They also used weapons such as home-made IEDs (Improvised Explosive Devices) to blow up tanks and armored vehicles.

" Kandahar is so remote, so far down the supply chain, that weird things would happen. Like all of a sudden there's no laundry detergent… Or for two weeks, guess what? There's no soap. I remember it being very difficult to keep your clothes clean…

The climate down there in the desert is just brutal, and that's when they fight down there, in the summer months. They put it to sleep in the wintertime when the passes freeze over…

The food at the firebases is much better than the food in the rear… When soldiers come back from their tours on the firebases, you don't want to make them too comfortable. They do PT [Physical Training] all the time and the food isn't that great—wilted lettuce, a fatty piece of roast beef, and a cup full of instant mashed potatoes. When they go up to the firebases, they eat steak and shrimp. **"**

Captain Andrew Schmidt, 167th Airlift Wing, 451st Air Expeditionary Group, was sent to Kandahar as an executive officer.

LIFE IN AFGHANISTAN FACTS

- Afghan society is made up of many tribes and ethnic groups, with their own quarrels and rivalries.
- The United States made deals with neighboring Uzbekistan and Pakistan to use airbases for the operation in Afghanistan.
- Between 2001 and 2013, 1,729 U.S. soldiers were killed in Afghanistan.
- In December 2009, President Barack Obama announced a shift in U.S. war aims to create conditions that would prevent the Taliban returning to power once all U.S. troops withdrew from the country.

A U.S. Marine on a base in Afghanistan passes the time by reading a book.

Afghan Allies

The Northern Alliance in Afghanistan was made up of different ethnic and religious groups. They were against the rule of the Taliban government. Many were veterans of the fight against the Soviet occupation of Afghanistan (1979–1989). Their only unifying feature was their desire to topple the Taliban. The main leader of the Northern Alliance, Ahmed Shah Massoud, was killed on September 9, 2001, two days before the 9/11 attacks.

Coalition forces board a U.S. Army helicopter after a patrol hunting for al-Qaeda in the mountains on the Pakistan border.

Members of the Northern Alliance examine a bunker destroyed in a Coalition air strike in March 2002.

" It was good for us to work with them [Afghan National Security Forces] and to meet Afghans that felt strongly about the defense of their country… In the south it's a little easier to become discouraged when the only locals that you meet are insurgents or those supporting the insurgents. The Afghan National Security Forces were good and we worked with them very closely, from the officer commanding the Afghan National Army company and his counterpart, the battalion commander, down to the pile of soldiers that we were going on patrol together with. That part was very good.

With the Afghan National Police, there were some units that were very good, very fierce fighters… But there were certainly some of the district Afghan police at that time that were not very professional… They had a whole range, I guess, within the Afghan National Police, but the Army was fairly professional across the board. "

Captain Michael John Reekie, from Alpha Company, 1st Royal Canadian Regiment Battle Group, served in Masum Ghar in Afghanistan after the fall of the Taliban.

AFGHAN ALLIES FACTS

- The Northern Alliance is thought to have numbered between 10,000 and 12,000 fighters.
- Northern Alliance troops and U.S. Special Forces defeated the Taliban at the Battle for Mazar-e-Sharif on November 9, 2001, their first major success.
- Members of the Alliance followed a more moderate form of Islam than the Taliban.
- Alliance fighters were armed with Russian-made weapons and tanks.
- Al-Qaeda suicide bombers killed Commander Ahmed Shah Massoud in an attack linked to the 9/11 attacks.

Special Forces

Using local guides, a Special Forces detachment prepares to move into Afghanistan in late 2001.

U.S. Special Forces were the first Allied troops to enter Afghanistan. Operating in small groups, often moving around on horseback, they set out to win the support of local people. The Special Forces included fluent speakers of local languages, including Pashtun. Special Forces also helped to flush out al-Qaeda from a cave complex at Tora Bora in December 2001.

A Special Forces commando carries out reconnaissance in a valley in Afghanistan in February 2002.

66 As a Special Forces officer, to be on the ground in Afghanistan, especially after 9/11, hunting al-Qaeda and fighting the Taliban, it was supremely exciting. But we knew that things could go terribly wrong in a hurry there. I knew I could die there and it was possible they would never recover my body…

This was a very serious business, and at any minute we could have found ourselves fighting for our lives. Thinking back on our Special Forces training, however, I remembered what I learned at the culmination exercise of the Special Forces Qualification Course. It was set in a fictional country… we were working with guerrilla forces to overthrow the despotic government… [So] I had done this all before in training and we were as well prepared as anyone could be for this situation. **99**

Major Mark E. Mitchell, Fifth Special Forces Group, U.S. Army, was awarded the Distinguished Silver Cross for bravery at Mazar-e-Sharif in 2001.

SPECIAL FORCES FACTS

- The U.S. Army Special Forces, or "Green Berets," carry out unconventional warfare, using guerrilla tactics and "psyops," or psychological operations.
- U.S. Special Forces took just two months to unseat the Taliban at the start of the war in Afghanistan.
- Special Forces worked with the Northern Alliance to capture the strategically important town of Mazar-e-Sharif on November 9, 2001.
- Special Forces lost three U.S. Army Rangers and one U.S. Navy SEAL to heavy Taliban fire in the Battle of Takur Ghar in March 2002.

On Patrol

Parts of Afghanistan remained highly dangerous more than a decade after the fall of the Taliban. The most dangerous region was the southern province of Helmand, where British troops replaced U.S. troops in January 2006. The Taliban still had large numbers of fighters there. Patrols, carried out on foot or by armored vehicle, were vulnerable to attack by IEDs (improvised explosive devices). These home-made bombs were placed by the roadside and could blow apart armored vehicles. Foot patrols were also at risk from sniper fire.

A U.S. Navy Hospitalman hands crayons to a local child during a patrol in Helmand Province in 2012.

" Every job is dangerous out there. We secure the route. But as we found out, [mine detectors] only pick out eight out of ten IEDs. When it's a command pull, there's no metal needed… The only way you would spot them is ground signs. Rocks piled up, a change in the color of the sand. Dips in the ground or sometimes they would put water on top of where it had been disturbed…

It was quiet, but it was around evening time when [the Afghans] all eat, so nothing you could pick up on. I was in front. The IED went off behind me. People must have walked over it. It was a command pull, after the fifth bloke had gone over it. They targeted the Amercian, he was getting intelligence. We had three injured, including one walking. The American was worst… The guy I was dealing with had a broken arm, a few fingers missing and shrapnel wounds. He had been thrown down a ditch into a massive crater and couldn't walk. **"**

Adam Gunningham, of the British Royal Marines, recalls being ambushed on patrol by an IED.

PATROL FACTS

- Helmand is one of thirty-four provinces in Afghanistan; it is on the border of northern Pakistan. Both the Taliban and al-Qaeda remained active in Helmand.
- Helmand is the source of 42 percent of the world's heroin. Heroin is produced from the opium poppy, which is grown by local farmers.
- As of December 23, 2013, 447 British military personnel had been killed in Afghanistan.
- IEDs caused over 66 percent of all Coalition casualties in Afghanistan.
- Foot patrols were eventually phased out because they were too dangerous.

A convoy of heavily armed U.S. Marine Humvees patrols through Helmand Province in 2008.

Going to War in Iraq

The politicians who led the war in Iraq: Vice President Dick Cheney, President George W. Bush, and Secretary of Defense Donald Rumsfeld.

In the early 2000s, the war against terror turned to Iraq. The U.S. and British governments claimed that Iraq had weapons of mass destruction (WMDs); some people also thought Iraq supported al-Qaeda. United Nations (UN) weapons inspectors went to Iraq to look for WMDs, but a U.S.-led coalition attacked Iraq anyway in March 2003.

An Iraqi soldier stands guard as UN weapons inspectors leave Baghdad just before the Coalition invasion of Iraq.

❝ It was the middle of the night when they woke us up. We packed all our stuff up, and then right as we're getting ready to leave, someone had a radio to listen to the BBC… Then they just moved us out toward a strategic place in the desert that was a little bit closer to the border. Everyone drove in a long single-file column, and we did it at night. We were actually early…

Our mission was to go and secure the oil fields in the south, so I think we actually went over the border first… You could see the explosions. It was like a big thunderstorm without the clouds. You just see the flashes like that… The tanks were just going through and annihilating everything… They're shooting at the enemy, and they've got their turrets swerving, and you don't want to crash into a turret because it will take out the whole top of the ambulance. **❞**

Thomas Smith, Navy Hospital Corpsman, 2nd Tank Battalion, 2nd Marine Division, describes preparing for the invasion of Iraq on March 19, 2003.

IRAQ WAR FACTS

- After the end of the Persian Gulf War in 1991, United Nations inspectors located and destroyed Iraqi chemical weapons.
- In October 2002, the U.S. Congress authorized the president to use force against Iraq to protect the United States.
- U.N. inspectors led by Dr. Hans Blix were sent to Iraq to look for weapons of mass destruction (WMDs); they found no certain evidence of the weapons.
- On March 17, 2003, President Bush gave Saddam Hussein 48 hours to leave Iraq or face war. When Saddam ignored the warning, the invasion began.

The Army in Iraq

A female U.S. soldier searches the house of an Iraqi woman who is thought to be sheltering insurgents.

The army sent to Iraq was different from previous U.S. armies. The Secretary of State, Colin Powell, wanted to raise a massive army, but President George W. Bush would not introduce a draft. In the end, to meet the growing number of troops needed, reservists from the National Guard were sent to Iraq in large numbers.

" When we first kicked off the war in Iraq, the Army was moving faster than they had anticipated. So they were having problems keeping the forward troops supplied. They needed us to go in and resupply those forward-deploying, fast-moving troops. Because of how quickly everything was developing, they really didn't have an airspace plan for ingressing and egressing Iraq. There was a lot of traffic.

The first time we went in, it was during the daytime, which is unusual... It was daytime, desert sun. I saw a couple of Bedouins and a couple of camels up close. Some of the guys were waving... When we first went into Iraq, you'd see guys there in the desert. I remember thinking they knew what was going on. They might be out in the middle of nowhere, but they knew what was going on. **"**

Captain Brandon Taksa was a C-130 transport airplane pilot with the West Virginia Air National Guard.

ARMY IN IRAQ FACTS

- The Iraq War was the largest deployment of the U.S. National Guard since the Korean War (1950–1953).
- National Guard soldiers performed military duties on the weekend to keep them in a state of readiness for action.
- National Guard soldiers served an average 20-month tour of duty in Iraq.
- By June 2005, National Guard soldiers made up 45 percent of the total U.S. Army in Iraq.
- The United States led a coalition in Iraq, but was also willing to act alone.

U.S. Army soldiers fly home on a C-17 cargo aircraft after a year serving in Iraq.

Special Forces in Iraq

The first troops into northern Iraq were from the U.S. Army 75th Ranger Regiment. The Rangers' job was to capture key airfields at night so that a land invasion could take place. Special Forces took part in some of the major confrontations in Iraq. Their most famous single mission was the successful rescue of captured U.S. Private Jessica Lynch on April 1, 2003.

A Special Forces soldier fires a Carl Gustav rocket during a training exercise in the Iraqi Desert.

“ What a spectacular sight it must have been from the ground to see the silhouettes of hundreds of Army Rangers descending from the heavens and landing on that airfield.

With very little visibility and even less control of those old parachutes, accidents are bound to happen. As we plummeted to earth I literally found myself running on top of another Ranger's parachute in an event known as 'sky sharking.' I'm not entirely sure of the physics behind the reaction but two parachutes cannot stay inflated atop one another. I watched in helpless terror as his 'chute collapsed, sending him directly to the earth like a shot put. There was nothing that I could do.

When I landed I collected my parachute and removed my rifle from its scabbard… As quickly as I hit the ground I was moving. ”

U.S. Army Special Operations Medical Sergeant Leo "Doc" Jenkins, 3rd Ranger Battalion, recalls jumping into Iraq.

SPECIAL FORCES FACTS

- Around 1,000 U.S. Rangers and soldiers from 173rd Airborne Brigade parachuted into northern Iraq on the night of March 25/26, 2003.
- U.S. Rangers destroyed air-defense batteries around Iraq's main cities.
- Green Berets in Iraq used "psyops," or psychological operations, to win the "hearts and minds" of the Iraqi people.
- U.S. Navy SEALs captured the important Faw oil refinery in southern Iraq before the invasion started.
- The rescue of Jessica Lynch was the first successful rescue of an American POW since World War II.

Operation Iraqi Freedom

In March 2003, some 145,000 U.S. and British soldiers invaded Iraq. There was little resistance and the campaign was over in three weeks. The main opposition came from the paramilitary organization Fedayeen Saddam, which was loyal to Saddam Hussein's Ba'ath Party. Saddam fled, but many of his allies and family were killed or captured.

U.S. troops prepare to pull down Saddam's statue in Baghdad on April 9, 2003. This was the ultimate sign that the old regime had fallen.

U.S. Marines cover one another as they prepare to enter one of Saddam's palaces in Baghdad during the invasion.

" Incredibly, the looting had already begun. I saw wheelbarrows loaded with furniture, computers, heaters and fans, all being ferried to nearby trucks, waiting expectantly at the gates of government buildings. The most valuable "spoils" were, of course, taken from the palaces of Saddam and his sons…

It was around midday and the American tanks had arrived, just outside the hotel at Firdos Square, where a bronze statue of Saddam towered over all comers… A group of Iraqis—helped by Americans—set about bringing down the huge statue by tying a rope around it and using a tank to pull it down. When it fell, Iraqis cried out in happiness and immediately ran to kick it, and dance around pieces of the statue, their arms raised in the air. "

Ezzedine Said was chief editor for Agence France Presse. He describes the arrival of U.S. troops in Baghdad on April 9, 2003.

IRAQI FEEDOM FACTS

- Operation Iraqi Freedom began on March 20, 2003, when the United States launched Tomahawk missiles into Iraq from ships in the Red Sea.
- Casualties stood at 171 UN soldiers killed and 10,800 Iraqi soldiers dead.
- Saddam Hussein was captured on December 14, 2003; he had taken refuge in an underground shelter on a farm.
- The legality of the invasion of Iraq remains in dispute. Many people believe the war broke international law.
- Iraqis voted in December 15, 2005, to elect a democratic government for the first time since 1958.

Protests on the Home Front

Unlike during the Persian Gulf War, many people across the United States and Europe opposed plans to invade Iraq. Many people did not believe the connection the U.S. and British governments made between Iraq and al-Qaeda, or that there were weapons of mass destruction (WMDs) in Iraq. February 15, 2003, was a day of mass protests across the world. Millions of people in hundreds of cities marched to demonstrate against the imminent war.

Crowds carry banners at the antiwar protest march in New York City on February 15, 2003.

" I was among the antiwar contingent that swarmed Manhattan's midtown on February 15, 2003, a wintry Saturday. We spread across miles of city blocks, trundling past abandoned police barricades as we tried to inch toward the UN, where 10 days earlier then Secretary of State Colin Powell had presented what we now know was illusory intelligence about Iraq's supposed weapons of mass destruction.

The multitudes in New York were diverse and legion. There were anarchists and military veterans, vociferous students (I was then a freshman in college) and a motley cast of graying peaceniks—many, including one grandmother memorably puttering along in a wheelchair, had opposed American involvement in Vietnam. And there were myriad others: a band of preppy suburbanites with banners announcing themselves—'Soccer Moms Against the War'—musicians, street artists and workaday New Yorkers. **"**

Ishaan Tharoor, now a Senior Editor at *TIME* Magazine, recalled the antiwar march in New York City in 2003.

PROTEST FACTS

- Some 300,000 people took part in the New York march in February 2003. They wanted to march past the UN Building but were not allowed to do so.
- Large protests also took place in Chicago, Los Angeles, and San Francisco.
- In London, around one million people gathered outside the British parliament to protest the war. It remains the largest political protest in British history.
- As many as three million people marched in the largest rally, in Rome, Italy.
- Madrid, Spain, was the location of the second-largest rally.

Protestors in Washington, D.C. gather at the Washington Memorial, in front of the White House.

To attack Iraq is a war crime

The Iraqi Insurgency

After the fall of Saddam Hussein, the coalition's focus shifted to helping a new Iraqi leadership. Home-grown insurgents and foreign fighters destabilized the country. Sectarian violence grew from 2006 between Iraq's Sunni and Shiite Muslims. There were no major combat operations, but homemade bombs and suicide bombings became daily events.

A U.S. soldier from the 1st Infantry Regiment prepares to blow a padlock off a door during a search for insurgents in Anah, Iraq.

Insurgents in 2007. Many foreign Muslims joined the insurgency to fight on the side of the Sunnis or Shiites.

“ In the last room of the house the walls are lined with 155mm artillery shells, hundreds of them, and I felt the trip wire break as I kicked the door open… My first thought after I realized I wasn't vaporized was, 'I wonder what idiot wired this room up, what a putz.' Then slowly I backed out of the house and we all evacuated back to were we started that morning so the house could be control detonated…

We come into a house that all the windows have been taped up, so it's dark. We break into smaller teams so we can flood the house. I hear one of my younger guys screaming gibberish. My partner and I run to his aid and find he has two insurgents cornered in the same room he is in and everyone is screaming at the top of their lungs… Inside the house was a small weapons cache. My young Marine was lucky he was in between the insurgents and their weapons. ”

Petty Officer James Pell, H&S Company, 3d Battalion, 5th Marines, describes searching houses during a counterinsurgency operation in Fallujah.

IRAQI INSURGENCY FACTS

- Under Saddam Hussein, a Sunni elite ruled the Shiite majority in Iraq.
- Saddam's fall altered the power balance between the two religious factions.
- From early 2004 insurgency attacks rose from 25 per day to 60 a day by the end of the year.
- Around 80 percent of all attacks occurred in Sunni-dominated central Iraq.
- The number of serious bombings more than doubled from 2004 to 2006.
- On February 22, 2006, a bomb attack on a Shiite mosque in Samarra marked a new increase in the violence between Shiites and Sunnis.

The Troop Surge

U.S. soldiers in a Bradley Fighting Vehicle watch an air drop of supplies near Narhwan.

By January 2007 it was clear that a new approach was needed to end the violence in Iraq. President George W. Bush announced that a further 20,000 troops would be sent to Iraq. The idea behind this "surge" was that the more soldiers were deployed, the more likely a victory would become. By June 2007, there were 160,000 U.S. troops in Iraq and the strategy seemed to be working.

U.S. sailors use a rubber raiding craft to patrol a canal in Iraq in July 2007.

" Although most of the soldiers we worked with had good intentions, we knew that some of them were actually insurgents who were working for both sides. For them, it's just economics. They'll work for whoever is paying more that day, be it the government or the insurgency.

We learned to use that to our advantage: when the Iraqis were scared to be in a particular area, we knew there was a good chance an attack was coming. I learned that lesson my second night in Iraq. I was riding in a Humvee on a mission, and there was an Iraqi Army Humvee in front of us… It stopped and the driver refused to go any further, saying that the area was too dangerous. We had to keep moving… A few minutes later we were hit by a roadside bomb and attacked with rocket-propelled grenades and AK-47 fire. "

Captain Andrew A. "Drew" Fuller, U.S. Army Special Forces, spent 15 months training a battalion from the Iraqi Army.

TROOP SURGE FACTS

- U.S. forces increased by 30,000 in 2007. Iraqi security forces grew by 200,000 between 2005 and 2007.
- By the end of 2008, there were more than 500,000 U.S. personnel in Iraq.
- Americans and Iraqis worked together at security stations in dangerous areas.
- The U.S.-backed "Sons of Iraq" program paid former insurgents to cooperate with U.S. forces in providing security.
- More responsibility for security and governance was passed to Iraqi forces in anticipation of the eventual withdrawal of U.S. troops.

Medicine and Nursing

In Iraq, casualties were transported by helicopter to a field station for emergency surgery. The most seriously injured patients were flown to military hospitals in Germany, where the U.S. Army had the latest medical facilities. U.S. nurses and doctors treated many Iraqis, as well as Americans.

Soldiers from the 86th Combat Support Hospital transport a patient on an All Terrain Vehicle.

" The critical care unit of the hospital had three wards: one ward for Americans, one ward for Iraqis and one ward was for overflow. Along with critical care patients, we also did recovery of surgical patients. Each ward consisted of ten beds. The beds were similar to Army cots that were on wire frames at waist level. The foot and head were able to lift up. We placed orange mattresses on them for added comfort. The beds were very narrow, about three feet wide. These narrow beds were extremely difficult for patient turning. There were no safety rails.

We cared for patients in a very small, confined area, cramped with critical care equipment like ventilators, suction machines, etc. Nursing was a challenge. I received patients from other FOBs or directly from the field. They always arrived via a helicopter. The helipad was adjacent to the hospital… I don't think any of the nurses were aware of the extent of the traumas that we would receive or care for… We cared for hundreds of brain injury patients. Our supplies were always limited. **"**

Linda Miller served with the 228th U.S. Army Nurse Corps reserves in Iraq from December 2004 to December 2005.

HEALTH FACTS

- Medics carried tourniquets in their backpacks to treat casualties in the field.
- Brain injuries accounted for more than 20 percent of all injuries because of the increased use of IEDs.
- Nurses and physicians served a year-long tour of duty.
- Helicopters were used to remove patients from the battlefield.
- If necessary, a patient was stabilized and transferred to Germany within 36 hours.

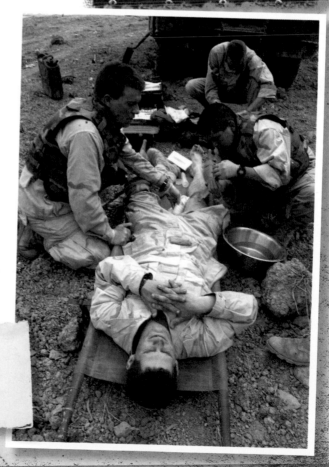

A U.S. Navy Hospital Corpsman treats a U.S. Marine for a gunshot wound to the leg after a firefight with Iraqi insurgents.

Recreation

Soldiers served for 12 months in Iraq. During that tour of duty they had a two-week break away from the war zone. The rest of the time, soldiers who were not engaged in combat had a lot of time to fill. In Afghanistan and Iraq, soldiers spent their leisure time writing and reading letters and emails, watching TV, listening to the radio, playing cards, reading, or playing sports when the temperature was cool enough.

U.S. soldiers on a base in Kandahar, Afghanistan, watch Superbowl XXXVI on a live broadcast in February 2002.

A U.S. Navy Seabee relaxes with a laptop computer and a cell phone.

" When it gets really hot on our off days, we like to swing by the pool. Yeah, that's right, there is a pool here. Chlorinated and clean, we swim almost once a week. For the brief couple of hours at the pool, you 'almost' feel like a civilian again.
Guys here will do all sorts of crazy things so that they don't forget they are human… I like to put on a baseball hat and forget that I should be wearing a helmet. It's the little things that keep us sane…

Everyone likes to keep in touch with their families and friends, so we have a couple of 'internet/phone centers' on the FOB [forward operating base].
You can use calling cards and talk to your family and friends, or you can log onto the computer and type an email, or check out some milblogs [military blogs]…

Like I've said before, we do a lot of odd things to pass the time. Lighting things on fire, playing with knives and swords, and causing all sorts of destruction and mayhem. We are just like a bunch of schoolyard boys. "

Taylor Allen Smith was a U.S. Army reservist who wrote a blog, American at Heart, while serving in Iraq in 2005.

RECREATION FACTS

- The USO (United Service Organizations) ran centers in Iraq and Afghanistan.
- The centers were "a home away from home," with free Internet, calls home, and recreation services.
- The actor Bruce Willis made morale-boosting visits to military bases in Iraq at the end of 2003.
- Soldiers were able to follow the progress of the war on American news channels that were broadcast in the camps.
- Afghanistan and, particularly, Iraq were the first conflicts when computers and cell phones were widely used by soldiers to communicate with home.

Defeat of Saddam Hussein

Within three weeks of the invasion, the Iraqi government had collapsed and Saddam Hussein was in hiding. The toppling of his statue in Baghdad was seen as the symbolic end of his regime. The city fell into a state of anarchy, as Iraqis looted former palaces and government buildings. Saddam was not captured until December.

Young civilians in Baghdad pause during the looting that followed the fall of Saddam. U.S. forces were not prepared for the outbreak of lawlessness.

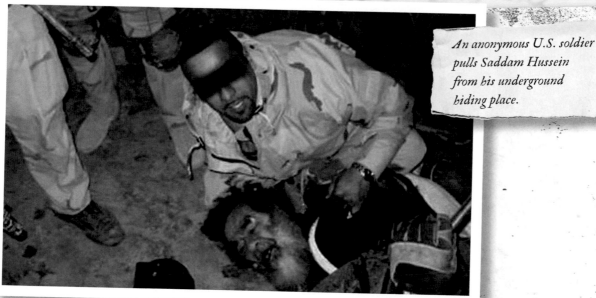

An anonymous U.S. soldier pulls Saddam Hussein from his underground hiding place.

" There's a guy in Baghdad right now who is a baker. His entire life he's been making bread for the Iraqis. He's seen his people suffer. He knows that when the Americans came and he watched Saddam's statue fall, it was the happiest moment of his life. He remembers looking over and seeing American tanks and Americans handing out water. Then he turned around and saw American soldiers dying, in his country, by the hands of insurgents who are not from his country…

He trusts the Americans and he knows they are there to help and he doesn't leave. He stays there every single day, while there are car bombs going off in front of his shop. He trusts that the Americans are going to help him get his country back on its feet. **"**

Weapons Sergeant Jeffrey M. Adamec, 3rd Special Forces Group, describes how Iraqis looked to U.S. troops to maintain order.

FALL OF SADDAM FACTS

- Saddam Hussein was the fifth president of Iraq; he ruled as a dictator from 1979 until 2003.
- His ruling Ba'ath Party belonged to the Sunni minority.
- Saddam Hussein went into hiding after the Coalition invasion. He was captured on December 13, 2003, hiding in a hole in the ground on a farm.
- The Iraqi government put Saddam on trial for the murder of 148 Iraqi Shiites; on November 5, 2006, he was sentenced to death.
- Saddam was hanged in prison on December 30, 2006.

Withdrawal from Iraq

The massive U.S. troop surge in 2007 brought the Iraqi insurgency under increasing control. But protesters at home continued to argue that the war was unlawful, and the Western presence in Iraq remained unpopular. President George W. Bush accepted the need to end U.S. involvement in the war and Barack Obama made it an election pledge in 2008. All U.S. troops left Iraq by the end of 2011.

> " Dozens of bases with American names that housed thousands of American troops have been closed down or turned over to the Iraqis. Thousands of tons of equipment have been packed up and shipped out. Tomorrow, the colours of United States Forces-Iraq—the colours you fought under—will be formally cased in a ceremony in Baghdad. Then they'll begin their journey across an ocean, back home.
>
> Over the last three years, nearly 150,000 US. troops have left Iraq. And over the next few days a small group of American soldiers will begin the final march out of that country… Those last American troops will move south on desert sands and then they will cross the border out of Iraq with their heads held high. One of the most extraordinary chapters in the history of the American military will come to an end. Iraq's future will be in the hands of its people. America's war in Iraq will be over. "

Transcript of President Barack Obama's address to soldiers at Fort Bragg, North Carolina on December 14, 2011.

WITHDRAWAL FACTS

- President George W. Bush and Iraqi President Nouri al-Maliki announced in 2008 that all U.S. troops would leave Iraq in the near future.
- In August 2010 President Barack Obama accelerated the end of the war and declared that the combat mission in Iraq was over.
- All U.S. troops left by the end of 2011; the war had lasted nine years.
- More than 4,400 U.S. military personnel had been killed in Iraq between the 2003 invasion and the eventual withdrawal in 2011.

A U.S. Command Sergeant shakes hands with a Kuwaiti border guard after crossing out of Iraq in December 2011.

The Hunt for Osama Bin Laden

Finding Osama Bin Laden, the head of al-Qaeda, had been the main objective of the United States since the attacks of 9/11, 2001. He was eventually killed in a Special Forces attack on his compound in the town of Abbottabad, Pakistan, on May 2, 2011. The attack was the result of intensive intelligence gathering that had led to the discovery of his whereabouts.

President Obama and military and political leaders watch a live relay of the operation in Pakistan from the White House.

" I started to wipe the blood away from his face using a blanket from the bed. With each swipe, the face became more familiar. He looked younger than I expected. His beard was dark, like it had been dyed. I just kept thinking about how he didn't look anything like I'd expected him to look. It was strange to see such an infamous face up close. Lying in front of me was the reason we had been fighting for the last decade.

It was surreal trying to clean blood off the most wanted man in the world so that I could shoot his photo. I had to focus on the mission. Right now, we needed some good quality photos. This picture could end up being widely viewed, and I didn't want to mess it up. Tossing the blanket away, I pulled out the camera… The first shots were of his full body. Then I knelt down near his head and shot a few of just his face. "

Mark Owen, a member of SEAL Team Six, recalls the mission to kill Osama bin Laden. Owen photographed bin Laden's body as evidence of his death.

BIN LADEN FACTS

- Abbottabad is located 100 miles (160 km) from the Afghan border.
- Bin Laden's compound had been built in 2006; he lived there in great secrecy.
- The operation to kill Bin Laden took 40 minutes from start to finish.
- Bin Laden was killed by a gunshot wound. Cameras in the helmets of the Navy SEALs filmed the whole operation.
- Three men, including a son of bin Laden, were killed, as well as one woman.
- Bin Laden's body was removed from the compound by the SEALs and later buried at sea. Al Qaeda confirmed his death on May 6, 2011.

GLOSSARY

bunker A reinforced underground shelter.

chemical weapons Weapons that carry harmful chemicals such as gas.

coalition A temporary alliance of countries or individuals to achieve a particular purpose.

draft A system of selecting citizens for compulsory military service.

extremist A person who holds extreme political or religious views and will use violence to support them.

guerrilla A soldier who fights by unconventional means, such as ambush, sabotage, or terrorism.

improvised explosive device (IED) A homemade bomb that is used in ambushes and booby traps.

insurgent A person fighting against an invading force or a government.

morale How positive or negative a person or group feels about achieving a particular task.

psyops Tactics designed to win support for one side in a war or reduce support for the other side.

reconnaissance The military observation of a region in order to find out about the location of the enemy.

regime A government that rules by force.

sectarian Supporting a particular group in a narrow-minded way.

strategic Related to the overall outcome of a campaign or war, rather than to the result of an individual action.

ultimatum A demand which, if it is not met, will lead to war or other retaliation.

warlord A military commander who does not answer to a higher authority.

weapon of mass destruction (WMD) A weapon that can harm large numbers of people at the same time.

FURTHER INFORMATION

Books

Carlisle, Rodney P., and John S. Bowman. *Afghanistan War* (America at War). Chelsea House Publishers, 2010.

Carlisle, Rodney P., and John S. Bowman. *Iraq War* (America at War). Chelsea House Publishers, 2010.

Gillard, Arthur. *The War in Afghanistan* (Issues that Concern You). Greenhaven Press, 2013.

Miller, Mara. *The Iraq War: A Controversial War in Perspective* (Issues in Focus Today). Enslow Publishers Inc, 2010.

Samuels, Charlie. *Timeline of the War on Terror* (Americans at War). Gareth Stevens Publishing, 2012.

Zeiger, Jennifer. *The War in Afghanistan* (Cornerstones of Freedom). Children's Press, 2011.

Websites

http://www.eyewitnesstohistory.com/cwfrm.htm
Links to numerous first-hand accounts from Eyewitness to History.

http://www.bbc.co.uk/newsround/15214375
A special BBC history of the war in Afghanistan for children.

http://www.pbs.org/wgbh/pages/frontline/terror/
Reports from *Frontline* on the War on Terror from 9/11 until today.

INDEX